The Empathic Parent's Guide to Raising a Highly Sensitive and Anxious Child

How to Talk to Kids and Empower them to
Believe in Themselves – 2 Books in 1

Freeda Meighan

Join Our Support Group

Finding a supportive community can be hard. Many parents feel like they are alone in their parenting struggles and that no one understands what it is like to raise children today. In order to make the most of your time and get more out of this book, I highly encourage you to join our active community on Facebook.

Don't be afraid to reach out. You're never alone in this journey, and these are excellent resources that can support you.

See you there,

Freeda Meighan

JOIN NOW

https://bit.ly/3zulOsI

Contents

The Empathic Parent's Guide to Raising a Highly Sensitive Child

Parenting Strategies I Learned to Understand and Nurture My Child's Gift

Freeda Meighan

Introduction

When Heather was growing up, I knew she was more special than other children. She was my eldest, and for a time, an only child. Since she was small, Heather was already a quiet child. I always thought she was mature for her age because instead of playing with other children, she was quite content sitting on her own, busy scribbling away with her crayons on a drawing board. We could even leave her alone for hours and she wouldn't mind. She was also very peculiar with noise. Whenever we would pass a mall with a blasting stereo, she would cover her eyes and cry. Heather would only calm down when we were back in the car, with a soothing lullaby in the background.

Heather was always particular about everything. I was quite exhausted at first because she had a lot of demands. She cannot eat orange foods or beans. She hated synthetic fiber and had allergic reactions when she wore wooly clothes. She had to be picked up at 4 PM after class or she'd fly into a rage. I was quite lost and angry at times because Heather would have tantrums and meltdowns in public when she didn't like something. From pleading to outright scolding, I tried to discipline Heather in the best way I could.

In my desperation, I sought the advice of a friend on what to do. She was a mother of my daughter's classmate and she could empathize with my dilemma. Her son was also very picky, and she was as lost as I was. But my friend told me to read about the "Highly Sensitive Person," a trait that she thought fitted my daughter very much. There were not a lot of resources, but I tried to read as many books and internet sources as I could. The more I read about highly sensitive persons, the more I felt that I understood Heather more.

From being insecure and lost about taking care of Heather, I began to see her more as a gift I needed to take care of. I began to accept Heather for who she is, an emotional and precocious kid who needed my help more than ever. I began to tolerate some of her eccentricities and particular needs but also made sure I didn't spoil her. In turn, I saw that Heather began to open up to me. From being a recluse and quiet child, she began to confide in me her little secrets and thoughts. In her little ways, she found ways to surprise me with her thoughtfulness. She still had her tantrums, but I was able to set definite rules, so she didn't have her way all the time. It was like cultivating a rare flower that slowly bloomed into beauty.

This book is an account of my journey with Heather. I now have two other kids and I have tried to treat them with the same love as I have for Heather. The insights in this book come from my personal experience of taking care of a highly sensitive child. I had a lot of errors along the way, but these errors proved valuable in teaching me lessons. Until now, I am learning a lot from taking care of Heather and I feel very happy seeing her grow before my eyes. I want to impart my knowledge on highly sensitive persons in the hope that more parents can readily identify the trait in their children and make the necessary steps in order to change the way they approach their children. Left to unguided hands, highly sensitive children can deteriorate, closing doors of communication and hiding in their shells. I want to build communities of care so that our gifted children will always feel that they are loved especially for their unique gifts. This book wishes to end the stigma against HSCs and what we can do for our children who may be gifted with sensitivity.

Chapter 1

Understanding the Gift

What is a Highly Sensitive Person (HSP)? One of the pioneers in understanding the trait of highly sensitive persons is Dr. Elaine Aron. She conducted research and came out with a book called "The Highly Sensitive Person," outlining the characteristics of these types of people. Through her extensive research, Dr. Aron was able to help a lot of people in understanding themselves with this common and yet not too discussed personality trait of being sensitive. Her work has spawned other research as many people began to be more curious about the topic and how people with this condition can be approached.

In terms of prevalence, Dr. Aron says that around 15-20% of the population is considered "highly sensitive." With a substantial percentage, HSPs are considered normal though not prevalent. This is important to note because the usual understanding of HSP is that being too sensitive is a disease or disorder that must be cured and be rid of. People who are highly sensitive may be seen as "too shy," "high maintenance," "too picky," or just unreasonably sensitive. Management of HSPs has been directed to a medical approach, as if being too sensitive can go away with a few pills. This is a gross misunderstanding of what being an HSP is. A reductive and narrow kind of thinking like this may hurt HSPs in the short and long run. They are a normal part of our population even though they may not fit the more popular or usual personality traits we know of.

An HSP is someone who has a heightened sense of their surroundings, who displays strong reactivity to internal and external stimuli, who has increased emotional connectedness and who has a predisposition to turn inwards. This definition may be difficult to understand but we can unpack these traits one by one. Bear in mind people you may know who have this or observe your children if you feel that they display some of these behaviors.

HSPs pay close attention to internal and external stimuli. These people have sensory receptors which are able to pick up much more sensation than normal people. This does not refer to any anatomical excess. HSPs are not people with more eyes, more noses, more ears, or more receptors in their skin than the normal population. Rather, these people have receptors that are more sensitive to stimuli. Their senses are heightened more than most people. For example, HSPs can be very particular to the smell of their surroundings. If normal people go to a room without noticing anything, HSPs may pick up certain smells that may not be apparent.

In terms of touch, HSPs can be very particular to skin sensations. In terms of clothing, some even develop hypersensitive reactions to certain kinds of fabrics. They can be very picky in what kind of clothes they wear because the clothes would be stimulating their body the whole time they are worn. Touch also includes temperature. HSPs are more sensitive to temperature changes, either feeling too cold or too hot when the rest may not complain. The reaction may be manifested dermatologically at times. Still on the subject of touch, HSPs can also be more sensitive to movement. They may be more alert when there is sudden movement near them, like when a ball comes directly at them, or a person suddenly hugs them from behind. They are filled with a rush of adrenaline as though they are being attacked. They can also react too readily, running away at the slightest movement or moving to a defensive position. They do not like anything that will disturb their routine and composure.

Sounds are a particular concern for HSPs. They can perceive sounds and noises more prominently than most people. Music that is usual for us, may already be too loud for them. Certain beats which may be engaging and may even prod us to dance may be too violent or strong for their tolerance. Because of these excesses, HSPs are most likely to retreat from loud and sudden noises, preferring silence or calm music. There is a greater tendency for them to avoid high-traffic areas, parties, rock concerts or packed crowds. They may want to go to a supermarket when there are fewer people. They may live in quiet neighborhoods or a vacation in secluded off-beat tourist sites.

The sense of sight is a concern for HSPs. They are more particular in terms of the things they see. It may be an overreaction to the particular hue of an object, the brightness or darkness of a particular shade or simply the arrangement of patterns and colors on a landscape. They are actually good at artistic endeavors because of this sensitivity to details. But it can also be very tedious for them to have multi-sensory stimulation. Flashing or strobe lights may tire them easily. Flashy or neon colors may be too strong. They may even just prefer to rest in somber-colored interiors or plain walls so that their eyes can rest.

Inward stimuli are also very prominently felt by HSPs. They have a lower tolerance for pain than most people. A pinch may be slightly irritating for some but excruciating for HSPs. An upset stomach may warrant an immediate consult at the emergency room. HSPs easily consult for medical help when they feel sick or are in pain. They are very much in touch with how their body feels and will voice out concerns at the slightest pain. They are quick to recognize if their stomach is killing them, if their head is throbbing or a lump is bothering them. They are good patients because they will seek help at the onset of the disease.

These external and internal stimuli are magnified in the HSP. They will encounter a lot of problems because other people may not be as sensitive to these stimuli and may think that their concerns are too trivial to be taken seriously. Not many people will understand their concerns out of ignorance of what their condition is.

Next, HSPs are also very emotionally connected. They are in touch with their emotions and will display them more prominently than most people. Even with little stimuli, they can easily be ecstatic, saddened, angered or frightened. Their power to empathize with other people and situations is magnified as if the pain of others is also theirs. They may be too affected because of the stories they hear or movies they see. Events in their lives may also be heightened to the point of trauma. An unfortunate incident such as an accident, sickness or death may cause them to be deeply scarred or depressed. They may feel personal responsibility or guilt when negative events unfold.

Their reactions to these emotional upheavals may also be exaggerated, both in manifestation and duration. If the rest are just sad, they can be sobbing or inconsolable. They are the loudest to shriek at horror movies, or they may avoid watching it altogether. They may feel so much anger inside them, but they are more prone to restrain themselves, imploding silently. What other people may feel for moments or days will become weeks, months, or even years for HSPs. They may hold a grudge for a very long time, be affected by a sad story for weeks, or never recover from the death of a loved one. They feel as if these events have just happened recently, with the details ever fresh in their minds. But in one sense, they can also be advocates for causes. If they feel strongly about particular interests and concerns, they are going to make themselves heard. They will feel passionate about personal issues and rally people to support them.

Finally, HSPs have a tendency to adopt an inward approach. They prefer to reflect on their own or think of things longer and more thoroughly than others. They may be described as antisocial or shy because they would rather mull things on their own. They are more introverted, listening to their own feelings and tuning out the feelings of others. Instead of seeking help from outside, they are going to nurture their feelings and grapple with these on their own. They would prefer silence, not just because of the lack of auditory stimuli, but more because of the solitude required for thinking and reflecting.

Again, these observations on HSPs may not apply to everyone. Not all HSPs are shy but most would prefer to draw inwards. Not all HSPs may be sensitive to light, but most may have a certain sensitivity to a particular sensory stimulation. Each HSP is unique and different, expressing their sensitivity in their particular ways. You yourself may notice some hint of HSP in you, if not an outright HSP.

What causes people to become highly sensitive? A study by Acevedo, et al. (2018) has focused on a genetic-based trait called Sensory Processing Sensitivity which is more developed in HSPs. In this study, they were able to map out brain circuit patterns among people with HSP and compared it with the brain circuitry of those affected with Autism Spectrum Disorder, Schizophrenia, and Post-traumatic disorder. Results show that all these four conditions stimulate the precentral gyrus, a part of our brain that is involved in the conscious movement. Also, the caudate, thalamo-cingulate and default mode network which includes the temporal, parietal and angular gyrus were similarly activated in HSPs. These centers are responsible for reflective thinking, motor and cognitive control. This anatomical correlation may explain the fact that HSPs are more inward-looking and self-reflective, sensitive to their actions and the feelings of others.

But what distinguishes the sensory processing sensitivity in HSPs from the other pathological mental disorders is the activation of brain structures responsible for hormonal balance, calm, empathy, self-control and self-reflective thinking. This is an important distinguishing factor because HSPs are commonly mistaken to have schizophrenia or autism. Rather than having a scanty, loose memory as in schizophrenia, HSPs in fact have a good grasp of memory. They are also able to integrate their emotional, cognitive and sensory system unlike people with autism who tend to lack emotional intelligence. We emphasize here the fact that the anatomy of the brain of HSPs dictates the kind of behavior they display.

Understanding what being a highly sensitive person means is crucial in our approach to people, especially to children with this personality trait. They are not meant to be cured in the sense of taking away parts of their personality that may seem inconvenient for us. We have to understand that they are normal people who have a particular personality that is not shared by the greater majority of people. Their very anatomy dictates their difference in thinking, feeling, and behaving, so that they are inclined to be more sensitive than others. Future research is needed to understand the highly sensitive person in fuller detail. I hope I have given you an understanding of the topic of "highly sensitive person" and before we move on to the next chapter, I want to let you know that in this book, I will focus more on Highly Sensitive Children (HSC) and what you can do now so that they can thrive as adults in future.

Chapter 2

Celebrating the Gift

With such a personality trait, what should our approach be to HSCs? If we have a child that is highly sensitive, should we see his or her personality as a gift to celebrate or a curse we need to break? It is very difficult to raise children who are highly sensitive, especially if we do not have that personality ourselves. It is hard to understand their behavior because it does not fit in with the rest of society, that they will always be viewed as pushovers in schools and reclusive monks despising social relations. Having a highly sensitive child may even lead us to question ourselves, if we did something wrong during the pregnancy, if we raised them up too spoiled or too left to themselves, if we were bad parents.

The key here then is a radical perspective on HSCs, to view them not as a curse, but as a gift we should celebrate, discipline, handle and nurture. A "gift" is a good metaphor to describe HSCs because they should be sources of joy rather than disappointment, anxiety, or even fear. Gifts are blessings meant to make us happy, the kind of happiness that is not fleeting or fake. As parents, we never know what kind of children we will receive and so it is with HSC as gifts. They are not accidents in a pregnancy outcome or a product of poor child discipline at home. They are gifts that parents receive and should be celebrated, as with any child that is born. They may have some peculiarities, but it is those peculiarities that make them special.

It may not seem easy for parents to view their highly sensitive children as kids, especially if they become difficult to handle. But they are children nonetheless who just have different triggers and needs. In the course of trying to manage a high-maintenance child, you might overlook the fact that they have certain talents, abilities, and dispositions which are unique to them and will bring you a different kind of joy. The HSC changes the family dynamics, even binding the family together because of their unique capacity to tap into the emotion of people. They are heart people, wearing their emotions on their sleeves. And this is a good jumping point to highlight the special gifts and talents of highly sensitive children. I will now highlight some of the more prominent gifts highly sensitive children possess.

They Are Patient and Keen Listeners

It is actually not hard to discipline HSCs. You may be surprised by this because you may think that they are just simply high-maintenance children. On the contrary, HSCs are good listeners and followers. They have great respect for their parents and authority figures and will follow commands to the rule. This comes perhaps from their need to please people and satisfy that need to be seen as doing what is right. They may also be afraid of being punished. Older children who are highly sensitive turned out to be very responsible in taking care of their siblings. Even without your supervision, they will follow what you say. In that sense, they are actually low maintenance because they are easy to discipline.

Their listening ability is also uncanny for children their age. Since they are very particular to sound and emotions, HSCs would pick up all the details of whatever you say to them. If you tell them that you will pick them up at 5 PM, be sure to pick them up at the exact time because they will listen and follow exactly what you said. They are listening not just to what you say, but how you say things, and the underlying emotions embedded in each statement. If you tell them, "Honey not now," they will know if you are tired, angry, annoyed, or simply not in the mood by how you say the phrase. They listen to the small nuances of things said and unsaid and this is a good trait. They are able to sense how people are just by listening to them.

They Excel in School

In general, HSCs do well in school. The academic setting is a place where HSCs thrive because their skills are honed in this setting. School pushes students to be attentive and particular to details, expressive in language and methodical in logic. These are areas where the HSC does well. School also wants to develop independent learning; hence students are given a lot of homework or personal activities to test their skills and abilities. HSCs love this because they can be on their own, concentrating on the work and putting much thought on each item. Subjects such as arts, language, reading and comprehension are fields where they excel because they have good attention to detail. They know how to mix colors and copy images on paper. They are particular to expressions in language and their memory is extensive. But they will also do well in Science and Math. The thought process involved in logic is something HSCs can be known for.

HSCs would encounter challenges to education when it comes to collaborative work and time management. They would prefer to work alone, but the school will often have activities that are team-based. School also trains children to work with each other, whether in projects or academic papers. And HSCs would have a hard time jelling in with other children because they have a particular way of doing things. They would either hog up all the work or have minimal participation. Their attention to detail is also something that can be tiresome for them. They can be perfectionists, unable to move on until the details are all perfect. And this can be time-consuming. The work is excellent, but it will take a lot of time. HSCs then won't thrive in time-pressured activities and exams because they like to take their time. But in general, HSCs would regard teachers as their ally and will excel in the school setting.

They Have a Sense of How People Around Them Are Feeling

HSCs will also be very sensitive to you and your family members' feelings. They can pick your emotional thermometer through your words and actions, and even the things you don't say and do. If you had a bad day in the office, they can sense right away and will steer clear from you. If you are generally happy and carefree, they can also sense this and will warm up to you easily. If you need a hug, they can sense that and will hug away all your pains and problems away. HSCs are very endearing children with high emotional intelligence. They can anticipate appropriate behavior based on the feelings projected to them.

HSCs then also make good friends. They can easily navigate the complexities of friendships and feelings. They know when their friends are fighting with each other, when they are developing crushes, or when they are having heartbreaks. They are the go-to-person when it comes to complex personal problems because they are able to analyze situations and empathize with people very easily. They can dish out advice that is grounded on sound judgment. They are patient listeners, able to sift between the emotions people feel when they tell their stories. With their keen observance of people, they can spot personality flaws and probable causes of problems. People depend on HSCs for advice, making them the best friend you always wanted to have.

They Are Quiet

This is actually a rare gem to find among children and a practical gift you can be thankful for. Unlike other children, HSCs are inward-directed and will require a lot of silence. The silence is a space for them to gather their own emotions, listen to their body, allows them to imagine and create their own world. They are good listeners and observers of people because they are silent enough to let their senses work optimally. This does not mean that they are antisocial. They will relate to others and even be talkative at times when asked. They just have a preference for being quiet, and active when needed.

As children, parents appreciate this silence because it creates a calm atmosphere in the house. People are able to relax because HSCs demand calmness in silence. They may be prone to tantrums and meltdowns, but these are rare occasions and often triggered by a particular concern. But for most of the time, they can be depended on to learn quietly, listen attentively and think independently. If you are not comfortable with silence, then this could be a problem for you. But silence itself is a gift you should explore and even inculcate in your own life as parents. You will do well to learn from your highly sensitive child how to be quiet yourself in order to be more self-reflective and attuned to your feelings.

They Are Very Thoughtful in Creative Ways

Being good listeners and emotionally connected, HSCs are also very thoughtful. They spend a lot of time composing what they want to say and usually, these are emotional statements that are well-thought-out. They can give honest compliments to people they appreciate. They are able to say negative things in a constructive way because they put effort into not hurting people with words. They will anticipate your needs and please you even before you ask for them. They are the ones who usually write cards on your birthday or on occasions such as Christmas, your anniversary, or Mothers' or Fathers' day. When it comes to their siblings, they want to make sure everyone feels good and appreciated. They will go to lengths to buy gifts for their siblings or to encourage them to do well in school.

HSCs are also very creative children. Give them paint and they will draw, a guitar and they will play, singing lessons and they will perform. These creative activities rely so much on attention to detail which they are good at. They love colors and are experimental on how they can make good drawings and patterns. Their inner world is also powerful due to their imagination. This helps them create characters, paintings, music that is novel and interesting. The punch comes when they use art to channel their feelings. If they feel angry, they may displace this in a canvass. If they are ecstatic, they can burst into song. They are not afraid to show their feelings and talents. When you notice their interest, develop that further because they are going to thrive in that area.

Chapter 3

Handling the Gift

It is true that we must appreciate our highly sensitive children as gifts and celebrate their talents and abilities. But these gifts also come with a few challenges. Like any other child, HSCs will also have their mood swings and personality quirks. Again, I emphasize that all children will have certain difficulties, whether it is in behavior, attitude, mental development, or communication skills. There is no perfect child all the time. Taking care of HSCs will be no different than handling a regular child who may be sweet at one time and then bawling in another. What we want to highlight here are some of the challenges parents may encounter when taking care of an HSC. Being sensitive people, HSCs will present with particular difficulties that parents should be prepared to handle. HSCs can be exhausting to manage especially if you don't understand what is making them behave the way they do. You may get frustrated with them, but by anticipating their meltdowns, you can conserve your energy and expectations better as well as become more patient with them.

HSCs Are Prone to Tantrums and Meltdowns

Sigmund Freud, the father of psychology, introduced the concept of the id, the ego, and the super-ego. He theorizes that all of us have these three components, influencing our behaviors. The id is the part of our consciousness that deals with our desires and wants. The id controls our need to seek pleasure. The super-ego is the part of our consciousness responsible for obeying rules and commandments. It is in direct contrast to the id which has no regard for conventions. The ego integrates the id and the super-ego together, deciding whether we should follow our wants or follow what is right according to social standards. The three components all work to influence what kind of choices we make on a daily basis.

HSCs are a furball of feelings and emotions. They are so in touch with them that they may have problems expressing what they feel inside. As children, they will be pure id, the part of our brain that follows the wants without regard for anything. If they feel anything, they will express it without being conscious if their behavior is appropriate or not. They may even create a scene in public when they get into a tantrum. It may be difficult to calm down, no matter how much you sweet-talk or even scold them. When the id is released, it will be very hard to control.

What are the usual things that set off HSCs? Each HSC will have a trigger unique to them and to the circumstance. They are easily affected more than other kids because they are so in touch with themselves and with their feelings. Any simple thing such as not getting the toy they want, not being allowed a certain activity, fighting with their siblings, a lost item they love, too much noise or any other extreme sensory experience may trigger a tantrum. Just like ordinary kids, HSCs will want to have their own way and have a hard time processing the different emotions they feel when they get rejected.

But what is particular to HSCs compared to other kids is the degree and length of time they can keep on having a tantrum or a meltdown. In terms of degree, their reactions can be rather exaggerated. Their fits can be disproportionate to the behavior they are reacting to. A simple "No" to their request can send them crashing on the floor. They will also take their time processing and feeling their emotions. If they are sulking from you, they will do so for a good length of time. They may not show their feelings on the external surface, but they may be nourishing a grudge for a long time. These meltdowns can even interfere with their daily activities such as school.

HSCs May Be Particular and Picky About Personal Items

HSCs have a certain way of proceeding and routine that they are particular to. They may fix their things in a certain way. They may have a particular way of eating their food or a particular texture of fabric they are comfortable with. They may be meticulous about the way they look or conscious of the brand of items they purchase. These routines are set and give the HSCs a certain sense of safety and predictability. If you disturb that rhythm, then you will really cross an HSC. If you mess up their cabinet or accidentally read through their private writings, then you will feel a lot of aggression from them. They have a strong sense of privacy and possession, taking good care of their things. If you cross their boundaries, then they will retaliate as though they feel attacked. They may even have a hard time trusting you a second time if you offend their sensibilities in any way.

Schooling may often be challenging for highly sensitive children. Though they excel in academics and individual work, the school setting itself may present certain difficulties for them. HSCs may have a particular way of learning or doing things that the teacher may not be able to provide. Socialization with other children will also be very tricky for them. Loud voices or strong personalities may antagonize HSCs, which influences class dynamics. Though the teacher cannot control all these factors, they should be guided as to how HSCs can learn better.

HSCs Have Difficulty Handling Negative Feedback

As with other children, HSCs will also commit mistakes. They may miss out on homework, may become unruly in class, or may exceed set video game times. As parents, your role is to discipline your children, giving feedback in a manner that is understandable for them so that they can stop doing behaviors you feel are not appropriate. The issue of feedback is very sensitive for HSCs. It is not because they are perfectionists who have high self-esteem and will take it hard if they commit mistakes. Rather, HSCs are so in touch with their emotions that negative feedback would be taken hard. You will scare them off if you suddenly burst into a raging sermon or even a wallop on their behind. They fear offending you more than anything. HSCs also tend to make things personal. When their work is deemed a "B+", they may also think that they are "B+" people, not good enough for the standards of teachers or of parents. They have difficulty separating their personhood from their work and output, so that an attack on their work is an attack on their person. You have to be careful then on giving them feedback. Deliberate well your choice of words because they need that feedback even if it is painful. But you can package it in a way that is less offending to them or will only focus on the output or behavior and not their person.

Giving feedback is as difficult for them as receiving feedback. Because they are easily hurt by negative comments, HSCs will also think of the other's feelings when they are giving feedback. They can spend hours crafting a feedback that is direct but not offending. They will expend a lot of effort, revising comments and approaches just to consider the other's feelings. In this way, they are very thoughtful. But the length of time they take to give out the comment may sometimes be too prolonged. It is actually good to get feedback from an HSC because you are sure that it is well thought out. But it will create unnecessary stress on the HSC just to give you the perfect feedback.

HSCs Are Targets of Bullying

With a heightened sensibility, a well-spring of emotions, and particularity with details, HSCs are easy targets for bullying. We see this very much in the school-age, where socialization happens with other kids. You cannot blame other children for not understanding HSCs because they are also exploring how they express themselves to others. But these interactions may often lead to abuses since HSCs may not fit in to certain cliques of children. They can be bullied for their peculiarities such as the way they dress, their fussiness on details, or seemingly weak characters. Some HSCs actually retaliate but that still opens the door for more bullying. Children are still finding their talents and abilities and exploring their social skills. HSCs also desire to belong to particular groups, but the school setting messes up with their preferred order of socialization. You have to be very vigilant in terms of observing for signs of bullying in your HSC. They can be verbally abused through name-calling or cursing. There could be instances of physical abuse when young people get out of hand. Rather than confide in you, they may just clam up and brood over their feelings.

It might also benefit us to discuss this bully-bullied relationship and how it can develop in school. I have to say that nobody is born a bully or a bullied. It is not a genetic trait that we pass on to our children. Most bullies are aggressive, but there are also cases of passive-aggressiveness that are as insidious as the direct ones. Bullying is brought about by the process of socialization, where personalities clash and aggressions are tested. Children are all different from each other, having different tastes and likes, looks, and origins. As such, diversity opens the door for the desire of some groups to establish a certain norm. This desire is very strong in teenagers where they want to belong to certain groups so they can fit in. If individuals don't fit into the standards set by the group, they can be antagonized through bullying. Bullies hate diversity and will desire only that their standards are the only ones to be followed. Bullies think that they have a monopoly on how to dress and behave, how to play games, and who gets to win. It is an issue of power, held by people who are just beginning to know who they are. The HSC, who epitomizes diversity, is the natural target of bullies because they don't fit in. HSCs are not part of the majority because they may be too shy or withdrawn into their own world. They have the capacity to retaliate, but the bullying may persist. The relationship between the bullies and the bullied persist because the bully draws power from overcoming the bullied. Once the bullied HSC realizes that he or she can afford not to give that power, then the relationship may be broken. When they stand up for themselves, HSCs are able to destroy the cycle of bullying.

HSCs May Be Secretive

The inner world of the HSC is the place where they feel safest. It is an environment where they can be themselves without being judged or pressured by others. It is both a thinking and an emotional space, a place where they brood over things they learned or process feelings which occur to them. You will find them mostly silent or staring dreamily into space as they are absorbed in their inner world. On the one hand, this is a good personality trait since it develops their sense of self-awareness and identity. By being self-reflective, they are able to get to know themselves better and plan out how best to interact with others. But on the other hand, the inner world may be an escape from encountering other people. When HSCs feel threatened, they are going to withdraw to their inner space, afraid to confront the stressor and resolve the issue. This is a coping mechanism they have developed because they have learned that by being silent, they can shut out the problems.

This will become pathological when the HSC encounters problems that they cannot solve on their own. Because they are naturally drawn to their inner world, HSCs can be secretive, nourishing their own thoughts and feelings to themselves. They will refuse to share with others their thoughts, feelings, and problems because they feel they are judged. If they have a problem in school, they will try to solve it on their own. If they have relationship problems, they will keep to themselves. If they are having issues with their gender and sexuality, peer pressure problems, issues with other family members, they will not open up easily. This is difficult because the problem at hand does not get discussed and is not solved immediately. Because HSCs are non-confrontational, sometimes, the problems become worse. You have to be very vigilant because the exclusive preoccupation of HSCs with themselves can already be signs that they are depressed or anxious, or even suicidal. They will only let you in if they trust you or if it is already too late. Watch out for danger signs when you feel that your highly sensitive child suddenly becomes secretive beyond the usual.

Chapter 4

Disciplining the Gift

It is good that we accept our highly sensitive children for what they are, affirming their skills and talents and providing them with opportunities for growth and self-awareness. This goes the same for any child that you may have. But, your duty as parents is still to form your children to become responsible adults on their own, capable of making well-discerned decisions and being able to function in all aspects of life. You still have to instill some form of discipline in your children, especially because they are still developing and capable of being molded. Being an HSC does not mean you have to give special treatments all the time. Yes, they have particularities that they are possessive of. But this does not mean you can simply tolerate excess or condone bad behavior. In fact, disciplining them may be the best way you can help them survive now and later on as adults.

I have formed some general guidelines on how to discipline your highly sensitive child. From the previous chapter, we note that HSCs have a tendency to deal poorly with negative feedback. But this is not an excuse not to give them what you think is right for them. Be courageous, because as a parent, you would want to equip your child with all the skills and resilience they will need when they become independent. Combine a lot of patience with gentle firmness so that you don't antagonize your highly sensitive child but still discipline him or her well.

Establish Rules

As with all your children, it is important for you to establish rules in the house. When you lay down the rules, you are teaching your children the value of keeping boundaries. These boundaries are not meant to make your kids uncomfortable or to repress their freedom. Rather, these boundaries are meant for them to enjoy themselves in the best and most productive way possible. Parents have a hard time establishing and enforcing rules because they also grew up in households that either have no rules or have too strict rules. Our own experience of house rules will actually determine the kind of rules we will enforce in our house. But since some of us have bad experiences of disciplining, it is best to understand what kind of rules will work best.

One quality of a rule is that it must be clear. When parents tell their children any rule, the rule must be very clear and delineated. If you tell your children that they should be home by night, they will be very confused. Does it mean that they have to be in the house when it gets dark? Can they stretch it to midnight? Is 4 AM still considered night? But if you formulate your rule as they should be home by 6 PM, then the rule becomes very clear. Rules that are vague will be subject to a lot of interpretations and you will end up becoming defensive and authoritarian.

The second characteristic of a good rule is that it should be reasonable. Your rule must make some sense, even to a child. The worst thing a parent can say to their children when asked why the children should do a chore is that "just because I say so." This is said when parents are exhausted to teach their children the logic behind the task or the chore they are being made to do. As parents, we should do our best to explain to our children why we do the things we do in the capacity that they can understand. When you tell them to make up their bed, you have to explain the value of cleanliness and having an ordered room and not just brush the question off with "Just do it." When they ask you why they have to stop watching television or play video games after an hour, do your best to explain to them the value of time management and even disconnecting from devices in order to interact with real people. They will not understand everything all at once. But when you are not defensive and children see that they can ask you questions without being brushed off, the following of rules becomes easier.

The final characteristic of a good rule is that it should be communicated clearly. You don't invent rules on the spot when it is convenient for you. You don't impose rules that only you can understand. These are quite self-explanatory, but you would be surprised at how poor some parents can be in explaining rules to their children. In their mind, they already know that they have told their children not to touch or use their personal items. But in truth, they have only mumbled it off in passing or explained it in vague terms. When their children tamper with their personal items, they fly into a rage and the children can get traumatized. You have to make sure that you state your rules in a manner that is understandable to your children. Ask them to repeat your rule after you said it. Test if they really remember your rules. You can only discipline them when they have understood your rule and still violated it. But until then, you cannot make them responsible for breaking rules you have not communicated properly.

The next part of establishing rules is enforcing them. You don't just make rules and not follow them up with execution. Rules are there so that the children will keep them. When you enforce rules, you have to be firm. They only become rules when children sense your authority in enforcing them. If you say the curfew is at 6 PM, then it is 6 PM, not 6:30 PM, not 7 PM. If you strongly feel that these are rules your children will need later on in life, then start them early with discipline.

Part of discipline, is, of course, making your children realize that their actions have consequences. Each parent will have their own style of disciplining their children in this regard. Some come from backgrounds where physical abuse such as spanking and belting are the norm. I do not judge the way you discipline your children. I will only recommend those that I personally feel worked with my own children and have seen it work on other children with better results. When you discipline your child, make sure that the punishment is proportionate to the task. When they commit a mistake, the consequence must be proportionate to the error. The power of punishment is when children can see that the punishment is graded according to the severity. If they fail in a subject, perhaps they are not allowed certain privileges until the next grading. If they get into a fight that resulted in being in detention, then they may not go out with friends for a month. These simple measures send a message that you are serious and that the destructive behavior of your children must be stopped. Also, allow for a system of warnings before you give a punishment. Give them a first warning for a first offense, a second warning for the next, and deal the punishment on the third. In this way, you are teaching children the value of second chances. Children will know their boundaries because they have been warned. But the most important advice on discipline is that you should communicate with your children. Explain to them the relationship between the bad behavior they did and the corresponding consequence. They need to understand or else they will keep on doing the same mistake while holding a grudge with you.

HSCs will need a good set of rules in order to behave properly. Like any other child, they will commit mistakes and break some rules. Try explaining consequences to them so that they can take negative feedback properly. Do not be soft on them because they will also need to be resilient at some point. Just make sure that your discipline is proportionate to the amount of learning they can get from the punishment. Remember that the goal of discipline is not to punish but to teach children how to behave properly.

Encourage Open Communication

HSCs are naturally withdrawn and secretive. But the behavior will only persist when they feel that they cannot trust others with their secrets or that they will be judged. If you establish a space where they can be safe and comfortable to be with themselves, then you will be able to enter their inner world. If you make this a general rule in the house where everyone has to abide, then your highly sensitive child will also learn to trust his or her siblings. Being open and honest with each other is a family culture that parents are responsible for establishing. When given the chance, HSCs actually like to share, especially if it is about feelings. They would want to share their feelings as well as get to know the feelings of others. In this way, your child will not have to be secretive and confide in others you may not trust. The whole family also benefits from open communication because there is greater bonding brought about by mutual trust and respect.

Allow open communication, especially when they commit mistakes. When children commit an error or break a rule, there is a tendency to hide it from parents because they will be punished. They may have experiences where you burst out in anger or you even physically hit them because they committed an infraction. Do not traumatize your children. There should be a healthy approach to committing mistakes so that you still get to correct the behavior but at the same, encourage open communication. Focus on the act that you want to correct and not on the person who committed it. Explain to your child that you are withdrawing privileges, not because he or she is a bad person, but because what he did was not good. By depersonalizing the behavior, you can still extend your love to your child and, at the same time, discipline him or her. The next time, children will feel that they can report to you their mistakes and own up to them. This already signifies that they are becoming responsible for their actions and are open to receiving the consequences. The corrective process then becomes formative for your children.

Involve Them in Housework

I found that doing housework is one of the foundations of a responsible adult. When you make your children do housework, you are building a character that will make them into responsible adults in the future. In a practical sense, this is convenient because you don't need to do a lot of things on your own. But at the same time, there is character formation going on when you involve them in housework. When children wash plates, make their beds, clean up after playing, throw trash in the proper wastebasket, you are instilling in them essential lessons they will bring to their own families and workplace. The house is the best place to learn hard work, good hygiene and etiquette, and good manners and self-discipline. Children will normally complain and you might be softened by their tantrums. But you are an adult and you have the power to mold them into constructive activities that will benefit your children in the future.

Housework is especially formative for HSCs. Involve them in household chores that they are capable of. They may initially refuse and go into tantrums. But once they see your insistence on the household chores, they will follow. From the following, they can learn how these small acts can benefit them as they grow in independence from their parents. Let them sweat it out as they clean their room so they can appreciate the value of hard work. Let them wash dishes so they can learn the value of hygiene. Let them pick up their toys and put them in the proper area so they can be responsible for taking care of their own things. When you do these chores together, you are even telling them that they are part of the family. HSCs can be self-absorbed and when they are drawn out by doing chores, they can realize how equally important it is to do things with other people.

Challenge Perceptions

Just because they are reflective and self-withdrawn does not mean that HSCs are always right. They may think a lot about something they learned in school or they may be bothered by a movie they saw and form an opinion about it. But it does not automatically mean that their opinions are balanced or even correct. They are children and they are still in the process of forming their own opinions, observing adults, and making sense of their world. HSCs have the advantage of being more introspective than their peers. But they may often times base their judgment and opinions on their own perspective. As such, the information they hold may be incomplete or even faulty.

To help them with this, encourage your highly sensitive child to expand his or her perspective. Do not tell them outright that they are wrong. Tell them that they can consider a different opinion or even an opposite one. If they strongly despise a classmate, challenge that opinion by telling your kid to look at the perspective of the other child. If they have strong opinions against a certain movie or dislike a particular teacher, challenge them by guiding them to think about the other person's feelings. In this way, their opinions are still their own but have expanded in terms of variety. By encouraging them to take the perspective of the other, you are actually drawing them out of their shell and into a healthy relationship with other people.

Coordinate With School

Make your child's school your ally. HSCs are prone to be bullied and you cannot be there the whole time to watch over them or to ward off their bullies. In this regard, the school becomes the second parent and has the responsibility for your children while they are in the vicinity. In order to help your child, get feedback from your child's teacher. The teacher is the best person who knows your child because he or she sees your child most of the day. They know class dynamics and how your child copes with the different stresses. They are then in the best position to give objective feedback on your child. They will also report to you if your child is being bullied and how he or she is handling the situation. The goal here is not to put a camera in the classroom but to seek out an ally in forming children.

Educate your teachers about what a highly sensitive child is. This is not to demand special treatment or even to make teachers pity your child. You should also be an advocate in letting other people, especially teachers, know about this particular personality type. When they understand HSCs more, teachers can actually cater their lessons so that HSCs can learn optimally. You can explain to your teacher that the child learns better by using pictures or that they are particular about loud noises. But you have to trust that teachers will do their best to educate your child as well as other children. The teacher is not just caring for one special student but is taking care of the whole. By educating teachers, you are giving them as much information as you can to help them see the whole class and to create a safe environment where children can learn.

Chapter 5

Nurturing the Gift

—ele—

Highly sensitive children have been described to be orchids compared to other children who are dandelions. This means that HSCs thrive only in certain controlled environments and will wither when placed in harsh spaces. If you push them too much in going to sports and playing basketball with their peers when it is not their interest, you will only isolate them and crush their spirit. If you only let them do the things that they want to do, then they may become spoiled and dependent on you, unable to function in other aspects of society without your presence. A good mix of loving discipline, firm guidance, and relaxed patience will certainly make your child bloom. Here are some points to consider when you are beginning to appreciate and nourish the gift of an HSC.

Accept Them

The best way you can ever take care of an HSC is to accept your child unconditionally. Tell them that they are beautiful, inside and out. Hug them constantly and make them feel special. When HSCs feel that they are accepted, they will become their best selves for you. When you love them unconditionally, they will want to love you back and others too, with the same openness and respect as you showered them. This may be rather obvious but often, acceptance is not the first instinct of a parent with a highly sensitive child. They can be confused with the gift, exhausted by their tantrums, and even critical of their thoughts and opinions. When you begin treating your child as a problem to be solved, they will remain unsolvable and elusive. Your child will be more guarded with you and will not open up their feelings to you because they feel threatened. Give them the acceptance that you also give to your other children.

In accepting the gift, do not compare it with the other gifts. If you have other children, nothing is more hurtful than comparing them to each other. If your older child excels in sports and the HSC does not, do not tell them to be more like their older sibling. This comparison game is unfair to everyone and sets standards on your children that they do not need and harms their own growth. Your HSC will bring this into their adult lives, debasing themselves because they are not enough for you and will not be enough for any other standard. They will inherit this comparative behavior and repeat this deforming attitude to their own children. Stop comparing your children. Tell your HSC that they should just be more of themselves. Your children are all different from each other, though they may look the same. What binds them together is your unconditional love for all of them. In this way, the HSC will learn to appreciate their uniqueness and will not be ashamed of being different.

Establish a Routine

Create a schedule you can follow on a daily basis. For example, you can set a wake-up time for 7 AM. Your children should be making their beds, brushing their teeth then shower up afterward. Breakfast at 8 and off to school. Pick up kids at 4 PM, free time until dinner at 7 PM. Wash plates, have a shower, and off to bed. Routines. You might not appreciate the power of routines especially if you have an erratic schedule. But routines are valuable to HSCs because they give them a sense of control. The predictability of the breakfast in the morning, the assurance of school, the fixedness of bedtime all give a sense of calmness in a highly sensitive child. Because they know which activities will happen at particular times, they feel relaxed and are able to be themselves. There is even anticipation of events which makes them excited if they like that activity. They can prepare for exams or tests that are routine, so their stress level is controlled. Routines make for a good disposition and good preparation.

When you disturb the routine, they can get flustered and lost. Surprises in the routines can be very stressful. The stress abates when they find a familiar face or event. If you miss picking them up from school at 4 PM, they will start panicking. If they stay up too late at night, they may be sleepy the following day. If you need to leave suddenly for a business trip which they don't know, they can feel very uncomfortable. Small glitches in the routine may foster some sense of resilience as HSCs are forced to deal with the situation. But prolonged unpredictability can cause them severe stress they may not be able to cope adequately. Routines then are very therapeutic for HSCs.

Encourage Their Interests and Talents

HSCs are one of the most creative and talented of personality traits. Because of their attention to detail, to the way colors are mixed, to the composition of images and the progression of notes, HSCs are natural artists. Encourage them to explore their talents by enrolling them in workshops, buying them art tools and crafts, bringing them to museums. Children are at an age where they need constant stimulation. The mind is still very plastic and will develop only to the extent that it is used. So, good exposure to the arts may open creative channels for your child. They may not exhibit good artistry at first, but by mere exposure, they may grow into the creative process. Encourage your child if he wants to play an instrument, write a short story, take good pictures or dabble in clothes-making. It is exciting to care for an HSC because a genius may just be in front of you.

Not all HSCs, of course, will thrive in the arts. Interests of HSCs can be as varied as sports, math and sciences, wall climbing, engineering, skateboarding, or computer programming. Each child will be as different from the other but support them all just the same. You or your child may initiate the exploration of an interest. The more that you expose your child, the more information he or she has of what he or she is good at or wants. If your child has a strong objection to a particular activity, don't push them too hard. You may want your child to thrive in a particular field, but if that is not what he wants, then he will do poorly in it. As parents, we can only help our kids in exploring their own passions. But we cannot make them passionate about something by forcing them on it. Let them discover who they really are on their own guided by our loving support.

Respect Their Personal Space

If you have taught them the value of boundaries in house rules, also be respectful of the HSCs own personal space. As introspective people as they are, HSCs will be very territorial when it comes to their space, whether physical or emotional. The personal space gives them a sense of calmness and peace because it is a place where they will not be judged for being themselves. This is a space where they can mull over their feelings into its fullest extent. You may be very concerned about what they are thinking and feeling. But you have to give your children the space where they can be themselves without your prying. Yes, there is open communication in the family. But there should also be spaces for private thoughts and feelings. You may be invited to this inner space, but you cannot force your child to divulge all of his secrets.

Respecting personal space involves protecting a safe distance from the common space to your child's place. Do not read your children's diaries because that is theirs. Do not eavesdrop on their conversation or stalk them at school to see if they have friends you trust. Stop being helicopter parents always snooping at your kids. They will tell you when they feel that they can trust you, not when they are threatened to be honest. Trust is not something you demand from your children, but rather, something you earn, even if they are just children.

Involve the Whole Family

Unless you are a solo parent, the joy and burden of raising a highly sensitive child do not depend on you alone. There is great joy in sharing the challenges and genius of HSC with others. As a couple, it is not only the mother who has the task to take care of the child. Both mother and father are equally responsible for disciplining their children as well as enjoying their company. You or your spouse may be working. But you should also learn how to balance your work with taking care of a highly sensitive child because the attention demand may be higher in them compared to most kids. When highly sensitive children are throwing tantrums and you feel too exhausted to the point of screaming at the child, stop yourself and let the other partner take over. When you are too busy to attend school activities, involve your other half so that the child still feels attended to. This delicate flower only grows when both parents are there to make him feel loved.

The dynamics of siblings are also a factor in raising a highly sensitive child. If your child is an only child, then they may have a tendency to be absorbed in their inner world and deal only with others during school. But when they have other siblings, HSCs will have to interact with them, adjusting themselves to each other's temperaments and personalities, getting into fights, and enjoying games together. Involve your other children when you are taking care of an HSC. It is not so much giving special attention to the point of neglecting the other children. You just want to make the other children aware of their sibling's particular needs and to be more conscious of them. The HSC is a gift to everyone because they can tap into the emotions of the family and bind them together. When a family works in harmony to take care of a highly sensitive child, they are brought closer to each other and become more sensitive themselves.

Chapter 6

Growing With the Gift

At this point, you may have some idea of how to take care of your highly sensitive child. They are challenging to take care of, but the rewards far outweigh the stress. When you see your child thriving in school or confiding secrets with you, there is a sense that you have done something right in raising your kids. Celebrate those moments because these are times when you become affirmed of your calling to become parents. Seeing them grow is like harvesting the fruits and enjoying a well-earned bounty.

But your highly sensitive child will not always be a child. They will grow into their own persons, choosing their own careers, picking their own partners, starting their own families, and living their own lives. As parents, you can only be there to support them when this happens. Our duties as parents never end but only change from an active to a supportive kind of parenting. We are partly responsible for their adulthood because the way we take care of them as children determines the kind of people they will become. But HSCs, in general, will have specific challenges in adulthood they will encounter. By knowing these challenges, you can anticipate what kind of preparations you can do so they will be equipped to conquer these challenges.

Becoming Independent Adults

The issue of self-dependence is very real to adults with HSCs. Two extremes in parenting may develop two extreme forms of attachment in adult HSCs. If the parenting type is very cold and distant, where the parents are hard on discipline and cannot tolerate the tantrums of a highly sensitive child, then the adult HSC may become as cold and distant. They will have difficulty opening up to other people because their own experiences of family and parents have not been enriching. They will grow up as mistrustful of other people with low self-esteem because they have been subjected to much criticism growing up. Some, of course, are able to resist this pattern, but only with much effort. The destructiveness of a cold parenting style will traumatize the HSC until adulthood.

On the other hand, if the parenting style is more of spoiling the child, giving them whatever they want all of the time, then no discipline is learned. Adult HSCs will become very dependent on their parents who have become their sources of consolation and safety. When they feel stressed, their parents will solve problems for them. When they want luxury, their parents will provide for them. When they need something, their parents will be at hand. When the parents are less able to provide, the adult HSC will be mortified that he or she has to face life on his own. The adjustment to adulthood is difficult because they are used to being provided and cared for. It will take some time before they can establish themselves outside of their parents' identities.

The sweet spot is knowing the balance between a disciplined parenting and a loving one, making it a disciplined loving parenting style. In this kind of setup, parents raise their children with a lot of unconditional love, providing for them in the measure that they can. But there is also a premium for discipline, where children are given boundaries and made to realize consequences for their actions. With a disciplined loving parenting style, parents will raise responsible adults who are independent and trusting of other people. They will know how to be intimate with other people, but they will recognize boundaries. They will replicate the kind of parenting you gave them to their own children. So, there is a big burden to really discipline and love your kids at the same time.

Establishing Intimate and Professional Relationships

We can never escape relating with others as we grow old. The family and school already set up this socialization process. When individuals transition to adulthood, the interaction evolves to include professional relationships and even intimate ones. After school, your children will have to take up jobs whether as employees, entrepreneurs, doctors, lawyers, or whoever they want to be. But those areas will still involve a lot of interaction with other people. As professionals, HSCs can bring a lot of connectedness in groups. They will do well in creative positions, art professions, or those that involve artistic expressions such as advertising. With their emotional insight, they will do well as counselors, psychiatrists, and medical professionals. They may not thrive too

well in professions that are too technical and lack a lot
of emotional connectedness. In terms of blending with
other people, HSCs must be able to give a good sense
of themselves, a solid grasp of their identity. They must
be aware of what they want, what conditions will
trigger their stress, what kind of work they can
tolerate, which personalities they can gel with. With a
good sense of self, the adult HSC may establish himself
as different from others yet comfortable with it. If the
HSC fails to become self-aware, then he will always try
to adjust himself to what others want him to be. This
can be a tiring process of trying to fit in which will
cause a lot of stress.

In terms of workload, HSCs must guard themselves in
terms of stress management. They have a tendency to
overwork themselves and this can cause burnout. If
you mix persona, family, and professional problems,
then they can burst and simply shoot off. In order to
prevent this burnout, HSCs must be self-aware as to
their limits and how to cope with stress once they feel
overburdened. They will naturally retreat to
themselves and this is their way of recharging energy.
They may not be the ones who like to party away to
unload stress but would rather have a quiet dinner
and a good sleep to get ready for the next day. Stress

management is needed for HSCs to thrive in the workplace.

Intimate relationships are also a concern for HSCs. They can rather be good at it because they have a good sense of the emotional connection with another person. They may fall in love easily and wear their hearts on their sleeves. But they can also be fooled easily when people take advantage of them. These rollercoasters of feelings can be exhausting for them and they may think twice when entering new relationships. People who have dated HSCs say that they are thoughtful and sensitive on the one hand but may also be demanding for others. Once an HSC finds a suitable partner, their energy goes into dedicating themselves to their partners and to the family they will form. They will always be the more emotional ones, whether that is good or bad at the moment. Through a lot of experiences, they may learn how to channel that emotional intuitiveness to optimal use in intimate relationships.

Mental Illness and HSC

The strong inner world of the HSC makes them susceptible to a lot of mental illnesses. They get stressed easily and maybe fragile in terms of receiving negative feedback. All of these stressors could easily pile up in their unconscious, multiplying by the minute in their mind. When they have reached their limit in repressing all these negative emotions, they become very vulnerable to a number of mental illnesses manifesting in their teenage years down to their adult lives. Because they are very secretive in nature, they may be prone to depression as they would want to keep their issues to themselves. For fear of offending other people, HSCs would simply mope over their frustrations on their own. This cycle of thinking negatively about the world, of others and of themselves becomes a loop in their mind. Without intervention, they can easily succumb to depression.

Since they are also very emotional, significant negative milestones can deeply affect HSCs. Deaths in the family, sickness, unfortunate events and rejections may be so ingrained in them they will have a hard time moving on. Their current activities may be hampered because of a trauma in the past. This leads them to be susceptible to post-traumatic stress disorder. Small triggers about the traumatic event can already set them in an exaggerated behavior which is often self-destructive. As adults, HSCs need to toughen themselves and watch out that their emotions don't control them and their social functioning.

Anxiety will always be marked in HSC. This stems from their bullied past, where they had to go to school and confront all those bullies. They simply graduate from school but in their adulthood, bullies and the bullied still exist. HSCs still take on the role of the bullied and the anxiety that comes with it. They fear being judged, they anticipate negative events, and they always think about a grim future, the HSC may succumb to generalized anxiety disorder. Through reasoning out and proper relaxation techniques such as returning to their routine, HSCs can cope with these life stressors and lessen the anxiety they work themselves up on their own.

It does not mean that being an HSC will make you mentally ill. There are a lot of HSCs who are able to cope well with stressors and live integrated lives. What I am saying is that given the nature of HSCs, they have a higher chance of acquiring these mental illnesses compared to the general population. HSCs must begin by understanding what ails or stresses them and find ways to cope in a healthy, life-giving way.

Conclusion

It is not easy to have a highly sensitive child who may have a lot of demands. You might be blaming yourself for producing a child who cries easily, who is frequently bullied or who goes into inconsolable tantrums. You may even think that giving them birth is a mistake. Stop worrying. Your dilemma is very much unwarranted and comes from not knowing who your child is and how beautiful and blessed they are. Having an HSC as a child is a gift you should treasure. Not everyone would want such a gift given the many complexities it possesses. But when you are lucky enough to have one, be thankful. There are many talents and abilities locked inside your child. They have a great power to connect people through a deep insight into their emotions. HSCs are very thoughtful and mindful of how people are feeling. They make sure you feel good and that the family is bonded together. Always remind yourself that having a highly sensitive child is a gift you should nurture and develop.

Hopefully, you have learned a lot about how to take care of your highly sensitive child. Remember that at the end of the day, you have to be patient with them. There is a slow process of formation happening each day. With your steady guidance, your highly sensitive child will bloom on their own. You may not see the changes right away or on a daily basis. They often bloom when you least expect it. Wait lovingly on your highly sensitive child and you will be rewarded magnificently. How you care for your child now will determine the kind of highly sensitive adult they will be in the future. So, invest in caring for them now and reap much joy as you watch them grow.

The Empathic Parent's Guide to Raising an Anxious Child

How to Help Your Kids Overcome Shyness, Worry, Separation and Social Anxiety

Freeda Meighan

Introduction

It was Heather's first day at school. We had been going over the details of today, but Heather was still hesitant to begin schooling. We had bought all of her crayons and drawing materials together. I let her personally pick out the type of bag she wanted. She wanted a cute pink bag with unicorn design, and she couldn't put it down all day. We also picked out her lunch box, pink again with fairies all over. She was all set for school. That morning, I woke up early to make her snacks. I packed her favorite Tuna sandwich, some breadsticks and an apple in her lunch bag. I even squeezed in a couple of chocolate bars. I woke Heather up and told her it was time to prepare for school. The look on her face was just one of utter horror. She just wanted to stay home. But the thought of using her pink bag eventually got her out of bed.

On the way to school, Heather was silent in the backseat. She was usually talkative during our car rides, but today, she kept on glancing at the windows, a look of apprehension deeply etched in her forehead. "Mom, can I start school next year?" she would ask me. "No, sweety, it's now or never." Heather wasn't too happy. Being the only child for some time, Heather was very attached to my husband and me. We were very hands-on in raising her. But growing up, we noticed that she was very sensitive to a lot of things. I actually talked about her in my previous book, "The Empathic Parent's Guide to Raising a Highly Sensitive Child: Parenting Strategies I Learned to Understand and Nurture My Child's Gift." Heather was a highly sensitive child, with a lot of special needs. But we adored her very much.

And now, school was becoming a problem for her. We arrived at the school and I wanted to just drop her and go. I needed to be at the office by 9 and I was already running late. I escorted her to the building and we admired the cool designs of the classrooms. Her room was at the far end. It was beautifully decorated with a lot of zoo animals. Her teacher, Mrs. Richards, was a kind looking lady and immediately welcomed Heather. I thought it would be ok because Heather had let herself be led to her chair. I was already walking away when I heard Heather throwing a tantrum. "I want my Mom!" She was making a scene and the other children were starting to get tearful. I had to go back to the classroom to reassure her. But

Heather just clung on to me. Mrs. Richards allowed me to stay for a while and enjoy the lesson with Heather. I was late, and I was stuck with my child who was mortally afraid of being left alone.

This scene may be very familiar to most parents. The first day at school is the most traumatic, as children are first exposed to a setting outside of home. I thought that the first day jitters were normal and would go away. But as the weeks went by, Heather still didn't let up her tantrums. Other children were already doing well in the classroom, making friends with each other. But Heather was still clinging on to me. After finding out about the highly sensitive person, I realized then that perhaps, she had a problem related to her high sensitivity. I researched, read a lot of books and talked to professionals. It was only then that I realized that my daughter was suffering from separation and social anxiety.

In this book, we will tackle the specific concern of separation and social anxiety, especially for kids who may be extremely shy and worried. I want to share my insights on raising a child with social anxiety to other parents who may be lost at what to do. The more that we know about our children's condition, the more that we will be able to respond best to their needs.

Chapter 1

Understanding Your Child's Anxiety

Each child we encounter will always be unique and incomparable. You may have four children and they could all be very different from each other. They have their own interests, likes, and dislikes, gifts and vulnerabilities, thoughts and feelings. Though they may share certain qualities, they cannot be truly comparable. Even the most identical of twins will have some amount of difference from each other. Being a kid yourself, you may have felt bad about being compared to your siblings as you state your own independence. And now that you have your own, it is good to first establish this uniqueness in every child. We can talk about them through certain similarities they have with others, but we cannot completely generalize their behavior.

And in dealing with stress, children will have different reactions. Some children thrive on it, seeing every problem as a challenge they can overcome. You may have experienced some children who are more daring than others, pushing the boundaries of social norms to state their own independence. These children can endure different problems from family and school and still come out strong. Some children may be slow to warm up. These children may be quite wary at first of an impending threat. But after gauging the safety of the environment, they are able to play and wrestle with the unknown. They may watch others first to see if the scene is safe and then proceed to play with others. And there are those with a low tolerance to stress. These are children who may be easily agitated or fearful when a problem comes up. Even at the slightest threat, they easily retreat to a safe zone or else tear up completely. Again, we have to say that children are unique and will respond to stress in different ways.

What then makes a child shy or anxious? There are several theories why some children are shyer than others. One perspective on shyness points out at a combined hereditary and social-upbringing factors as a cause. A child's disposition is usually inherited from their parents. The temperament of both parents or one of them can rub off on your child. If a mother is usually outgoing, has a lot of friends, goes out a lot, then the child has a higher chance of also being as outgoing. If the father is quite reserved and pensive, preferring to stay at home most of the time, then the child could also grow up as introverted. There are, of course, exemptions to this rule, but more or less, you can judge a fruit by its tree.

Second, modeling plays an important role in the process of socialization. Children always look up to their parents for everything, from the provision of food to being protected in a house and for their every other need. They look at their parents and try to mimic or copy their actions, thinking that it is what is right. The process of modeling works through observation and application. The child first observes the parent perform an action, and then tries it out for himself. When a mother says "Mama", the child will try to mouth "Mama." When a father blurts out a curse word, the child will also say the same, without regard if it's right or wrong. What the parents do, the child will also do. This modeling works to help children be eased into their social roles. A father demonstrates to his son how to ride a bike, play basketball, or tinker with a car. A mother shows her daughter how to sew a quilt, how to bake a cake, how to dress up for occasions. Shyness can then be seen as a product of a modeling scheme. When the parents try to avoid public places, the child will sense that this might be the right action and will mimic or do the same. If the parents are too worried to get out of the house, then the child will also imbibe that action as their own. This is not deterministic, as there are still some children who will develop their own behavior. But modeling is a strong explanation for shyness.

A third explanation for shyness points out a traumatic perspective of socialization. One negative event may have been imprinted on a child that he has generalized it to other situations. For example, a child may have encountered a stranger in a park while playing. The child may be initially friendly to the new child, even offering his toys. But the stranger may have hurt your child or stole his toys away. That memory may have stayed with your child. He was scared and hurt when he was trying to play with a stranger. In his mind, therefore, all strangers are not to be trusted. Negative events may have a stronger impact than positive ones. If we are not able to process these feelings, the child may nurture them for a long time and may convert that into extreme shyness and social anxiety.

There is no one formula to explain shyness and social anxiety. Different factors may be at work in the development of these behaviors. But we still have to deal with our children's anxiety. Yes, there are cases where the shyness is quite tolerable and we just have to let our children be. But sometimes, shyness can get in the way of your child's development. Because of social anxiety, your child may be afraid to go to school and that would compromise his education. Because of shyness, your child may need you to stay in the house at the expense of your work or your other errands. Then you create a problem of your own. It is imperative then to go to the root of the problem. We have to understand where the anxiety is coming from. If we want our children to develop well and to socialize confidently, then we must try to understand the anxiety behind the behavior.

Chapter 2

Signs and Symptoms of Anxiety

All of us experience some form of stress in our daily lives. Living in an imperfect world and interacting with different people, we are always prone and exposed to different kinds of stress. The intensity of stress will also vary according to the problem of each person. No two people will react to the same stress in the same way. Two students trying to answer the same Math problem in a test will have a different reaction to the stress. If one is more prepared, then there is less stress. But if the other has not really studied at all, then the stress level is greater. From simple morning traffic to the hassle of a long line, to more complicated problems like deciding to divorce your partner or experiencing death in the family, we all have our own experience and reaction to stress.

The Diagnostic and Statistical Manual of Mental Disorders V, states that anxiety is the anticipation of future threats. When we are faced with an impending stressful event, we experience anxiety. We may just be even thinking about a future event, and we are already anxious. On the one hand, anxiety helps us prepare better for the future. Because we are so concerned about an exam, we can prepare for it earlier by studying hard. When we are anxious about a business presentation, we review our material thoroughly beforehand. But on the other hand, anxiety can overwhelm us. Too much worrying can prevent us from doing our daily functions. Because we are so caught up worrying about getting sick, we don't go out of the house anymore. You are so anxious about speaking in public that you end up passing that opportunity for others to benefit from.

If there is such a thing as 'healthy' stress, the kind that helps us perform better, there is also such a thing as 'healthy' anxiety. But if the anxiety becomes pathological, then it will already affect our daily functioning. For a behavior or a thinking process to be pathological, two things are considered: the effect of the behavior on daily functioning and the duration of the behavior or thinking. One, we look at how anxiety prevents us from doing our daily functions. If too much worrying already prevents you from going to school or performing at work, then it is pathological. When the worry makes us miss family occasions or makes us neglect our health, then it is pathological. Second, the time duration is important. We will discuss different kinds of anxieties across the developmental age. The diagnoses of these conditions are only made when the behavior is evident for particular periods. Some diagnoses require the conditions to be present for at least 6 weeks, some for 6 months. The point is that the anxiety must exist for a prolonged period. We recognize that we can be anxious. But if we experience it unceasingly for more than a month, then we may have a problem.

Children too, experience all sorts of stress. Their concerns are totally different from adults', but the impact on their development is more profound. Children are just discovering their world and are entirely dependent on their parents. When they feel safe and secure with their family, they will seek to keep it that way. When they find their environment hostile, they will go back to the comfort of their family. They will start to meet other people aside from their family and that can be a difficult process of socializing. They will start to discover life outside their homes and for some that can be quite traumatic.

It is more difficult to diagnose anxiety disorders among children because most parents don't think of seeking help early. Some parents observe their children for long periods of time, hoping that their social anxiety will simply disappear. They keep on pushing their children into situations that they are not comfortable with, in the hopes that they will get over their own anxieties. It may work for some, but others will have bad memories of the experience. Some children will swim on their own if they are thrown into a pool, while some will drown out. And so, children never get the help they need at that stage. They will carry that childhood trauma later on into their adulthood, making them less functional.

I would just like to discuss in a particular way, the case of highly sensitive children (HSC). I have discussed this thoroughly in my previous book, but I feel the need to highlight their case in this instance. HSC feels anxiety much more intensely than other children. In terms of social circumstances, HSC will be more sensitive to the different sights, sounds, smells, tastes, and environment. They may not react to unfamiliar situations very well. It may take a while for them to warm up to others when they feel comfortable. It is important to understand how anxiety affects HSC because they are more sensitive to stress. You would need to guide them more carefully to become more resilient. Now, we are going to go over some disorders of anxieties children might experience.

Separation Anxiety Disorder

This disorder is seen mostly in children who are afraid of being separated from their parents and caregivers. A child is diagnosed with a separation anxiety disorder when he or she experiences at least three of the following symptoms:

Recurrent excessive distress when experiencing or anticipating separation from home

You will see these children really distressed when at the thought of leaving either one or both parents, depending on how attached they are to each other. They may cling on to them when they go out of the house, physically using their bodies to prevent you from exiting. Even just the thought of being actually separated makes them feel anxious already. We see this very commonly during the first day of school. There are some children who need their parents in the classroom for the first few weeks. They will cry and launch into a tantrum when their parents leave them. Eventually, some of them outgrow this and become comfortable with the school. But there are children who will still cry for their parents even after months of being in school. The separation just makes them more anxious.

Persistent worry about experiencing an untoward event that will cause separation from attachment figures

These children worry about different negative events that may happen to their parents. They are afraid that they will become sick and require them to be hospitalized away from home. Children feel that even cough and cold may warrant a trip to the hospital where they cannot go. They are anxious that their parents may meet with an accident on the road. They may sit in the car and are horrified at daydreams of experiencing an accident. They are mortified at the thought of losing their parents permanently. The thought preoccupies them and they need to see that their parents are physically ok before they can relax.

Reluctance to go out because of fear of separation

Going out of the house can be a daunting task for these children. Even the thought of going out the door mortifies them. Beyond the door, they feel very unsafe. They may consider the street and the neighborhood as foreign places. Parks, markets, schools, restaurants, and other public places scare them very much. They feel that the environment that is not their home is all dangerous places. Perhaps, they may have bad memories of these spaces, so they generalize it to other places. Because of the previous trauma, they are afraid of going out of the house.

Persistent fear of being alone without attachment figures

Socializing will be very hard for these children. They may always need the presence of their parents when they are interacting with other people. In family gatherings, for example, they may also be at the back of their mothers, trotting always behind her. When left to themselves, or with other people, they already feel anxious. They will keep looking at the crowd, trying to see if their parents are there. Failure to locate them will result in a meltdown.

Friendships in school are also problematic. They are not family and so these classmates will become strangers to them. They may not be able to participate in group activities because they will always want to be with their parents. This may often be a cause for bullying as they are termed "mama's boy or girl" or "papa's boy or girl".

Persistent nightmares involving separation

Children may wake up in the middle of the night, having dreamt of being separated from their parents. They will have no control over the content of their dreams, but because of excessive fear and anxiety, they carry that over to their dreams. That is why most of these children sleep with their parents in the same bed and room even if they are old enough to have their own. They need to have the physical security of being with their parents during sleep. This might cause problems when one parent has to leave for some legitimate reason. The child then may not be able to sleep well because of the separation.

Physical symptoms

When entertaining thoughts of separation, or having the actual experience of separating, these children will feel all sorts of physical symptoms such as nausea, vomiting, indigestion, palpitations, and difficulty of breathing. Some of these reactions may escalate to an exaggerated level that necessitates a trip to the hospital. The physical reaction is also their way of making you follow their wishes and address their concerns.

Selective Mutism

At home, you may observe that your child is able to converse well with you and with other familiar figures. They have a good vocabulary and they are able to express themselves well. Among their friends, they are also able to speak well. They can trade jokes, share stories and speak about their experiences. Intellectual competency may also be normal. They may do well in school in terms of written exams. But when these children are tasked to speak in front of the class, they suddenly become mute. There is selective mutism at work when children fail to speak in specific social occasions where they are expected to speak. Perhaps, they are afraid of being judged for how they speak or what they are speaking about. They are afraid of being ridiculed and embarrassed. So, they simply shut up.

But when the speaking occasion passes, they are able to speak normally. You may need to assess with a professional when you notice that your child is selectively being mute.

Specific Phobias

We say that anxiety is felt when anticipating a future threat. Fear is specifically felt when you are stressed about a particular object or situation. This specificity is called a phobia. Some people are afraid of spiders and we call that arachnophobia. Some people are afraid of crowded places and we call that agoraphobia. Your child might have a particular object or situation where he or she is afraid of. In other circumstances, they function normally. But when faced with that specific trigger, they launch onto hysterical cries and palpitations. They want to avoid that stimulus as much as possible. Try to observe what specific object your child may be afraid of.

Social Anxiety Disorder

We say that a child has social anxiety disorder when there is marked fear or anxiety in being in a social situation where there is possible scrutiny from others.

These will include social interactions such as conversations with strangers, eating out in public, commuting, shopping, or just walking in a crowded area. They fear occasions when they need to perform in public such as a recitation, a play, or a choir. Such situations are really frightening, but for socially anxious children, they may experience these more intensely. They may react to it even in an exaggerated manner including crying, throwing a tantrum, freezing, clinging to their parents, shrinking o,r failing to speak up. They will try to avoid these situations as much as they can. They would rather stay at home than visit a mall. They may volunteer others for recitation instead of taking the opportunity. They may delay work just to avoid social interactions. They are not able to function well when they are forced into social situations they have no control of.

With all these symptoms of anxiety, it is important to determine the extent of the condition in your child. Are they exhibiting anxiety symptoms only to a particular object or situation? Are they ok in general but clam up on social occasions? How does the anxiety manifest? Is schoolwork compromised? Have the symptoms been felt for a long time? These are questions you need to answer when you make an assessment of anxiety disorder. You may need to refer to a professional to help you spot these symptoms and address them earlier.

Chapter 3

Effects of Childhood Anxiety in Adulthood

You may feel hassled now taking care of your children. And you might think that they can outgrow all of that on their own. Some parents are experimental and would rather have their children exposed to so many stresses until they are able to overcome them. Yes, there are exceptions, where some children are able to move out of their social anxiety. But most of them will have traumatic experiences of standing in front of a crowd, being in a public and open space, and commuting using public transportation. Instead of learning from their mistakes, these children will remember those memories as bad reminders of their own incapability. Some of these children are often introverted and may not open up easily. As such, the repressed memories may persist through adulthood and affect their development. This chapter presents some of the dangers when childhood anxiety persists and is not addressed. Without proper recognition of the problem and adequate response, your child may develop some of these problems in adulthood.

Function Impairment

The trauma that they felt during childhood may affect different aspects of social functioning. One, their school performance may be compromised because of bullying and repeated exposure to stress. In fact, these children may be so traumatized to go to school that they end up staying at home. Their academic learning is stunted because they are afraid of other people bullying them or the prospect of doing something in front of other people where they can be embarrassed. If they continue to go to school, their attention may be drawn more towards avoiding other people or social exchanges rather than on the subject matter. They may be actually good in Sciences or Math, but because they need to work in groups or that they need to recite in front of everybody, their fear takes over learning. Hence, their potential is diminished, rendering them less than optimal when they are already working.

Second, the social relationships they build may also be compromised. If they are not able to establish friendships or even good communication and social skills at an early age, then they will find it difficult to work with other people. They may instead gravitate towards jobs that are solitary and afford minimal interaction with people. But if they don't practice relating to others, it may be difficult for them to cooperate and negotiate with others. They may be brilliant on their own, but when they are communicating their ideas to others, they may be lost in translation. The work is compromised when they need to work with other colleagues.

In terms of intimate relationships, it is still possible for them to be able to date and find life-long partners. But the process would be very difficult. They will have problems trusting other people because they have bad childhood experiences of relating to peers. Perhaps, they are going to look for other people who may resemble their attachment figures or someone who is as recluse as them. It will take a while before they can find their own friends and partners on their own. In terms of parenting, they may be the types who worry a lot, and that can translate to their unique parenting style. If they are not able to overcome the shyness and worry, they can easily transmit those characteristics to their children.

Medical Conditions

Social anxiety may also lead to certain physical symptoms. When you have a panic attack, you may have difficulty breathing, palpitations, headaches, nausea, and vomiting. There is less oxygen flowing inside of you and you will feel all sorts of pain. These are just acute symptoms related to stressful events. You feel these just as you are going out of the house or entering a public place. Usually, it would subside once the stressor has been eliminated. But for some, these reactions persist. When the conditions become chronic, you are prone to develop certain diseases.

With elevated blood pressure and palpitations, you may develop hypertension or other cardiovascular diseases. Stress actually releases certain hormones in the body that activate the body's fight or flight mechanism. When these chemicals persist beyond the required time, they can actually damage your blood vessels and organs. They may create harmful toxins that build up in your blood vessels, impeding blood flow. Thus, you develop hypertension. If you don't watch it, you are prone to clogging up vessels in your heart or in your brain leading to a heart attack or stroke. Do not disregard stress because it can actually contribute to the development of cardiovascular diseases.

Related to hypertension is obesity. When your kids stay home most of the time because they are afraid of the outside environment, the tendency for them is to eat and just sleep at home. Without much stimulus from the outside, they are going to be eating a lot of food, also to cope up with the stress that they feel. Sure, it may be negligible in childhood or even adolescence. But these bad eating patterns and sedentary lifestyles may induce your child to develop dyslipidemia or hypercholesterolemia. These are conditions where the excess fats consumed are stored in blood vessels. Over time, the fats will clog the vessels completely and compromise oxygen delivery. These may easily develop into other morbid diseases related to the cardiovascular system. Obesity will also make them less mobile. You also need to watch out for Diabetes Mellitus because of the junk food and sweets they consume. All of these will take a toll on your child when they become adults.

Mental Illness

Social anxiety will also predispose the individual to develop other mental disorders. The anxiety they feel may trigger other mental diseases when they are not addressed. We may not even be sure if the anxiety is the trigger or if it is a result of a pre-existing condition. But an individual with anxiety may have other mental conditions occurring at the same time. It is important for you to notice all the symptoms of mental diseases because negative consequences may occur.

One, individuals with social anxiety may develop depression. It is said that these two conditions, depression and anxiety, feed off each other. Because of the anxiety, you try to avoid people and the stressful environment. However, the isolation may also cause you to be depressed. In depression, you may have recurring negative thoughts about yourself, about the world and about the future. You may think that you are bad because you cannot relate well with others. For you, the world may be a toxic place filled with people who are out there waiting to embarrass you. And this cycle will just continue. Because of the depression, your sleeping and eating patterns will be heavily influenced, either in excess or in deficiency. The stress may cause you to overeat or to sleep less. You may feel tired most of the time. Your child will tend to withdraw to their safe zone and shield themselves from the world. They can just retreat into themselves and shut people out. When they do, it is hard to draw them back to normal functioning. The meltdown may take days and they may feel very depressed. Professional help may be warranted at this point.

Second, you really want to watch out for suicidal ideation and attempts from people with anxiety and depressive symptoms. We can see this among adolescents and young adults who are still in the process of managing their emotions. They have a lot of stress around them that they cannot fully process. It is good if they tell you these ideations because it means that they are open to being helped. But when they are shutting themselves from everyone, it is more difficult to help them. They are prone to suicide because they may just want to end the stress and the suffering they feel inside. They may think that they are worthless and blame themselves for everything. The sense of hopelessness pervades deep in them and the only escape is through suicide. Do not disregard any thoughts and verbal communication about suicide. Treat it as real and talk to your child. Do not wait until it is too late.

Lastly, having anxiety attacks may actually develop into personality disorders. The constant fear and anxiety may become more permanent and be the default way a person relates with others. With a sustained fear of others, a paranoid personality may be formed. This is where a person begins to mistrust everybody even without a good basis. They feel as if people are out to get them, plotting against them and talking behind their backs. They feel attacked most of the time even if in reality, that is not true. A dependent personality can also develop. This personality needs another person to function well. In their childhood, these children are highly dependent on their mothers and fathers. In adulthood, they will try to find mother and father figures that they can cling to. They cannot survive by themselves and need to depend on another person for their emotional needs. And an antisocial personality disorder can also develop. This would refer to a constant avoidance of all human contact. They want to be just by themselves most of the time, limiting all interactions with others. They will avoid circumstances that they will need to relate with other people. There are a lot more personality disorders that can develop when social anxiety persists. In all these, professional help may be warranted. So, try to detect signs of social anxiety early on to prevent other mental disorders from developing.

Chapter 4

Caring for Socially Anxious Children

It is not easy handling socially anxious children. Because of their particular needs, you would have to make a lot of adjustments. If it is your first time handling such children, you may feel overwhelmed and lost at what to do. As parents, we want the best for our children. We want to make them feel loved and supported. Seeing these children shy away from others may bother us. So many questions about how to raise them up or if the condition can be outgrown will pop into your mind. And all of this is normal. But now that you are able to recognize your child as having a heightened sensitivity, it is good to observe several guidelines when handling them. Unlike other children, you will need to exert extra effort to reach out to them. Here are some basic guidelines to help you care for socially anxious children.

Accept That They Are Children

First and foremost, remember that you are dealing with a child, not an adult. If you think that they can just outgrow their social anxiety on their own, you would be grossly mistaken. You might even be tempted to leave them alone in places out of frustration at their clinginess. This is terribly traumatic for them and will do them more harm. When you treat your children as adults, you are raising too high expectations of them. This will lead to more frustration for both of you. The child will try to please you by overcoming their fears to no avail and repeated failure while you will blame yourself for not raising your child well.

As children, they will need a lot of time and guidance to learn how things should be done. They are still developing and will be looking up to you for guidance. They will make a lot of mistakes. No matter how much you tell them that they shouldn't fear school or that it is safe crossing the street, they will still forget it and hold on tightly to you. Remember that they are very vulnerable at this stage. They are in the process of developing physically, mentally, emotionally, and socially. From the school-age years, they are going to discovering their talents and abilities, their limitations, and their capacities. They are still trying to find a way to fit in with others, constantly navigating the treacherous waters of socialization. They need friends but they might not know how. So, don't expect them to learn at the pace you want them to. They are kids still and will need some time to become confident and secure on their own.

But as children, their great advantage is really their eagerness to learn. They are curious about the world. But perhaps their fears and anxieties become so overwhelming that it paralyzes them. But if that fear and anxiety are addressed, there is a child inside who wants to play and be accepted for who he or she is. Your child may just have particular ways of learning about the world. Perhaps he doesn't like crowds too much or he hates noise. But children are very much willing to learn and discover the world. They have a thirst to know everything they could about the world. Perhaps other children are just more vocal about their intentions to learn, but yours is as curious. Capitalize on their childhood and their inexhaustible eagerness to learn, however peculiar their ways may be.

Highlight Their Giftedness

Before you can start complaining about how difficult it is to raise a socially anxious child, perhaps the first thing you should do is to find what is good with them. Many parents are so burdened that they may not realize just how good their children are despite their social awkwardness. They may simply focus on the hassle of raising a socially anxious child, on how annoying they can be when they cling on to you, or how difficult it is to send them to school. The frustration is understandable but let that not be the first and only thing that sticks to you when raising them up. Hard as it may be, find the good in each child and recognize that every one of them is gifted in their own way.

Even worry in itself may be a good characteristic, given it is in moderation. There is such a thing called 'good worry.' Because we care so much for something, we exert a lot of thought over making sure that everything is perfect for that event or person. When a child is showing signs of worry, it may also be that they are trying to be more careful. It could be a care for their own health and well-being. Their worry could be for you. They may want you to be safe and out of harm. In fact, because of the worry, you take extra precautions to be safe. In a way, this helps us second-check our decisions to make sure we are not making a mistake. The worry then is translated into productive anticipation of future events. Yes, that could easily be abused and exaggerated. But then again, not worrying at all could also be a red flag. A child who easily goes with strangers or does risky behaviors also puts himself in harm's way. It is actually more difficult to discipline a child who has his own mind rather than having one who is more on the careful side.

Social anxiety in children also masks their gift of obedience and listening. They are so fixated on you and will listen to your every word. As parents, you have to be grateful to have children who will listen to you and actually obey what you command them to. Discipline comes easy for these socially anxious children because their modeling instincts are still very intact. You can exploit this advantage by teaching them the values and habits you want them to learn. When they grow up, they will have a mind of their own. During childhood, you have a captive audience in your children. They are still malleable and trainable. Hence, our responsibility as parents to develop good morals in them is bigger during childhood. It may be grace then that they are still shy at this point.

And maybe, a little reassuring word may go a long way for these socially anxious children. We will discuss which power words to express to these children. But we need to empower them because most often, socially anxious children behave the way they do because they fail to see their giftedness. They may be good at drawing or Mathematics. They may excel in constructing intricate designs or manipulating tools. They may actually like reading and have a good vocabulary set. They may actually be good at teamwork or have leadership capabilities. But all of that disappears at the thought of performing in public or expressing those with gifts to other people. They fail to see beyond their fear and anxieties. As parents who can see the whole picture further, draw your child to see their giftedness also. Compliment them when they do a good job in school or at home. Display their artworks or hang their awards on a wall. Celebrate by eating out in their mini achievements. When socially anxious children are able to draw confidence from their achievement, they may be more secure to venture out of their shells. When they see that in other aspects they are doing well, they become more confident to share with others. Find your child's giftedness and use that as his strength.

One-step at a Time

As adults, we may be very used to multi-tasking. Once given a set of instructions, we have the ability to proceed on our own to accomplish the different tasks set before us. It is not uncommon to see people talking over their smartphones while typing on their laptops and squeezing a bite or two of lunch during pauses. We pride ourselves on being able to do many things at one time to show just how efficient we are. And it is very wrong for us to expect kids to be the same way. We cannot tell them to speed up on their tasks and make them do all sorts of activities all at the same time. They are not yet adults.

So, it is good to do things one step at a time. For example, your child may be very afraid of going to the market. It will be very traumatic for them if you just drag them over the grocery store and let them cry it out as you do your shopping. Instead of learning, they are simply overwhelmed by the anxiety and trauma you dealt them with. This is not a good way of teaching your kids. What you can do is a stepwise approach. Start by accompanying them to the door. Practice going in and out of the door until they are comfortable. Next, you can proceed with taking them across the street. It will be worrisome at first. So just gauge their level of comfort and then return to the house. The next day, try going to the other side. After a week, they can get used to crossing streets. Just inch your way day by day, week by week, until you are able to reach the market. It is tiresome and slow, but that is the only way they will learn.

Prepare Them to be Functional

What is good with children is that they are still in the process of becoming and learning. Unlike adults who are already set in their ways, children are still very much trainable. They can still adapt from their set ways given the proper instructions and modeling. It is actually exciting to teach children because their development is very dramatic. You can see day by day how they are able to move from mastery of one skill to the other. Today they start counting numbers from one to ten. The next week, they can already count up to 20. Before long, they can start adding simple numbers. And then, they will be able to subtract them. And so on. Socially anxious children are particularly enjoyable to teach because they pick up very fast. They are very focused on details and will obey you every step of the way. They like learning and when you start teaching them, they will absorb everything you say like a sponge.

Knowing this, we can say that it is possible to help your children outgrow social anxiety. They are still in the stage of learning and it is possible to learn how to socialize well. It must be clear to you that having them develop social skills is essential to their growth. You cannot just tolerate every tantrum they have and give in all the time. Just because you love them does not mean you will baby them forever. On the contrary, if you really love them, you should be firm in your ways to help them grow steadily from childhood to adolescence to adulthood in increasing maturity. They will need your help as children, but they cannot depend on you all their lives. You cannot be there for them all the time because you have a life of your own.

In order to do this, you must be able to play the roles of being a parent and a teacher for them. As a parent, you will endow them with unconditional love and support. As teachers, you should teach them by challenging them at an appropriate level. You should be able to balance supporting them as well as challenging them. You must be firm when you set rules for them. Don't tolerate tantrums as you would in any child. They will cry, but afterward, explain to them how their actions have consequences in real life. If they refuse to go to school, try curtailing some of their privileges like watching TV or playing with their toys. Explain to them the values of learning that they miss out on when they don't go to school. Teach them values in a way that they will learn from their mistakes. It is tedious, but it is the only way they will be prepared for life.

Family Is the Key

You don't need to do it alone. You may think that the burden of teaching and raising your child belongs solely to you. The impulse to shoulder everything is felt more intensely by single parents raising their children on their own. When you have this lone wolf mindset, you will easily get tired. When you start taking care of your children on your own, the tasks may even overwhelm you. Socially anxious children will have their particular quirks and needs that you will need to attend to. But you are not just a parent. You still have to do well at work and earn an income. At night, you may feel so tired but you still have to cook or check on your child's work. When your child has social anxiety problems, the burden becomes heavier. At some point, you may even be burnt out and may start lashing on your child unintentionally.

It doesn't have to be this way. If you are not a single parent, then you have your partner to rely on. If you have other children, it is the task of everyone to take care of each other. As parents, you take the lead in setting good examples for your children. But the other siblings can also teach their brothers and sisters. Make them feel responsible for each other. Share the burden with your partner. It is not a good practice to have someone focus on earning the income alone and letting the other deal with the children. You are both responsible for raising your children and not just putting money and food on the table. Strengthen teamwork and the load will be much more bearable for all of you. Social anxiety in children may not be common and people will need to adjust to your child's condition. Involve everyone in dealing with this challenge.

Seek Professional Help

Know that there is always help when you need it. Some parents may feel that it is their sole responsibility to raise their kids. But let's face it, we don't know everything. There might come a point when we really don't understand our children anymore. Rather than just letting them be, it is good to seek professional help. It is a misnomer to think that psychologists are just for crazy people. On the contrary, we all need some form of help and these professionals may give us that objective guidance we need in raising our children.

In the case of social anxiety, there are a number of specialists who may be able to help you. Developmental pediatricians and psychiatrists may be the most equipped in helping you deal with your child's social anxiety. They have studied the condition for many years and have developed a lot of research in that field. They may also have come across many other children and have helped other parents deal with them. Don't be afraid to ask for help because these professionals are entirely at your service. They may be able to suggest to you therapies that you can enroll your child in. They may teach you ways to deal with difficult children. And they may just expand your perspective on dealing with social anxiety. It is perfectly ok to ask for help. The earlier you seek it, the faster the problem is solved.

Chapter 5

Strategies to Support and Calm Your Child

It is important that you adopt the perspectives discussed in the previous chapter. These will help you prepare well for the daily management of your child with anxiety. It is one thing to learn about taking care of your child, and another thing to actually do it. There may be times when you will feel hopeless and tired after not being able to understand them. These strategies will help you take care of your child better. It will be difficult at first, but once you get the hang of practicing these daily, you will develop routines that will come easy for you. In all these strategies, it is important to gauge your child's reactions to everything that you do. How you will proceed will depend very much on your child's openness and willingness to learn and to change his or her thinking and behavior. Go slow and exercise a lot of patience and your child will slowly react positively.

Find a Safe Zone

The very first thing you need to do is to determine the safe zone of your child. When your child becomes very anxious about a stressful event, they are highly likely to experience a panic attack. They may become so overwhelmed with emotions and fear that they cannot think much anymore and will just let themselves be inundated with their feelings. Their reaction can also be exaggerated. This can range from simple crying and tantrums, or difficulty to move. But at its worst, physical symptoms may even warrant a visit to the Emergency room. With panic attacks especially, there could be feelings of nausea, vomiting, and difficulty of breathing. A simple trigger may send your child into a panicked state.

Instead of also panicking, the very first thing you need to do is to calm down your child. When they are panicking, they have less oxygen circulating in their brain and body. You need to help them breathe deeper and slower. Make them inhale and exhale deeply so that more of the oxygen flow in and the poisonous carbon dioxide be eliminated. You will see that they will calm down once they get enough oxygen circulating.

Next, you have to identify a safe zone. What is a safe zone? This is an area or an environment where your child feels most comfortable and at ease. This is entirely dependent on your child's preference. They may feel safe in their own bedroom or anywhere inside the house. They may feel that they are safe when you hug them or when they are holding a particular toy. They may feel safe when they have their headphones playing their music. They may feel safe when there are no people and there is less noise. Whatever it is, you have to identify that environment. When they feel stressed, you must be able to return to that safe zone. You want to remove that stress by returning to a place of comfort. This will help you establish a baseline that you can always return to. Children need to feel secure, so you have to respect that space. Let them retreat to their safe zone when they feel stressed. When they are calmer, that is the time when you can process their thoughts and feelings. And when you want to attempt to change their behavior, it is important that you let them know that they can easily run to their safe zone.

Develop Routines and Then Expand Them

Socially anxious children are very protective of routines. They like things that are predictable where they know what will happen most of the time. They have a great need for control especially when they feel stressed. They may follow particular routines at home, a specific time for waking up and sleeping, for meals and activities. Their things may be arranged in a particular manner and they easily know when something is missing or placed improperly. When they are able to follow their routines, they feel very much at ease and distressed. Of course, when that routine is changed even to some degree, then they will feel a lot of stress.

In real life, we cannot stick to routines rigorously. Yes, there are certain patterns of behavior we may be comfortable with. But it cannot be followed all the time due to circumstances we cannot control. A certain amount of resilience is needed. You need to be able to teach that resilience to your children in a way that is appropriate and understandable for them. You have to respect their routines, but at the same time, challenge those routines to help them develop resilience.

Two components are needed for this strategy. First, we have already discussed the safe zone. Children must be able to return back to their safe zone, so they feel calm and protected. In the case of routines, going back to their routine is a source of safety for them. So, you have to establish their routine and respect that. If they want to do their homework in a particular way that works for them, respect that. If they want a certain order to your shopping routine, just go along with that. They need to know that they can easily return to their routine before you pose a challenge.

Next, when you want to change their routine, the degree of change must not be too drastic. It must be different from their routine, but not radically strange. For example, your child is comfortable only eating meals at home. You noticed that anywhere else, they would clam up and not touch the food. In order to change this behavior, you have to introduce incremental changes to their routine. First, eat together inside the house. Your child will feel safe with this arrangement. Next, try eating outside the main house but still within your home. It could be on the porch or on a bench near the door. The child will still feel safe because it is still near your home and that they can easily go inside. But you already exposed them to eating at a different place. Next, you can try eating at a nearby restaurant or a breakfast place. It must be near your home so that they can feel comfortable. Expand the distance from your home at each mealtime over weeks. Do it slowly so that your child will not notice the changes very much. After a while, they will feel comfortable eating at different places. If you change immediately from eating at home to eating out at a restaurant, they may feel anxious and stressed that they won't learn anymore. The next challenge for you is to help them eat out in a different place without your presence, for example at school. For this, just follow the incremental changes in routine.

The safe zone and incremental change will help your child to change his or her behavior in a safe and comfortable way. Do not traumatize your child by making big leaps in terms of routine change. You can develop resilience in a controlled way. Of course, you cannot maintain that atmosphere when they become adults. There are a lot of factors you cannot control anymore, and they would have to do it for themselves. But at least, you are able to help them develop resilience slowly but surely.

Be Good Models

There are many ways in which people learn. Some people learn by reading a manual and applying the concepts after. These people like to understand everything in their minds first before they can apply what they learn. Some people learn by doing. They may not have any idea on how the thing works but they will just tinker with it and learn on the spot. This happens in the case of biking where there is no other way to learn but to simply bike. We all have our own ways of learning. Children learn things in a different way. Unlike adults, they cannot read manuals, or their limbs may not be equipped to handle things. Infants and young children learn by modeling. Children will look at their attachment figures and will copy whatever they do.

Modeling first works through the process of attachment. Infants observe their mothers first. They receive nourishment and milk from them, so they feel very secure with their mothers. Because they receive sustenance and unconditional love from their mothers, they will feel much attached to them. They feel safe around their mothers. That attachment is then extended to their fathers and to other caregivers. Children observe that when they cry and the father addresses the problem, by changing their diapers or feeding them milk. When they feel safe with that caregiver, they will also form attachments. The degree of attachment is highly dependent on the consistency of the positive reinforcement. When the child cries, the mother or the father should be there to calm the child down. When they are consistently present, attachment is very strong. But when there are prolonged times when the child is left unattended, the attachment will be very poor. The child will think that he or she can depend on the parents consistently. They will develop a tentative attachment, but with a lot of mistrust.

As they grow up, children will also refer back to their attachment figures. They regard their father and mother as perfect and will try to emulate them. When their parents eat, they will also eat. If they use spoons and forks, they will use those too. If they use chopsticks, they will also use chopsticks. They will constantly look to their parents for validation of their actions. The attachment can also become very dependent when the children have to constantly refer back to their parents for everything. Social anxiety is exaggerated when they are not able to form independent choices for themselves.

Given such an arrangement, your job is to be a good model to your children. If they see that you are comfortable meeting strangers, then they will also try to feel comfortable around different people. If you are also wary and have few friends, preferring to stay at home, then they will also be very recluse. If you like to engage people in conversation, then your child will also feel comfortable speaking up. If you are the type to also be very introverted, then your child will also be one.

Hence, you have to be the model for your child. If you want to change their behavior, you have to do it first and they will follow. If your child is anxious about going to school, be with them physically in the first few weeks. You cannot expect them to learn on the spot. They will still need to verify the safety of the environment with you. And when they become comfortable enough, that is the time when you can slowly disengage. But you cannot leave them hanging at the first instance. You will need to model and hopefully, your children will learn gradually.

Coordinate With Schools

It is important for you to coordinate with the school regarding the special needs of your child. For some parents, they would rather home-school their own children or send them to special schools. This has its own pros and cons. But you can still send your child to normal schools provided that you maintain close coordination with the school. You are not asking the teachers to do special favors for your child when you coordinate. You want to explain the circumstances of your child so that the teachers can gauge the kind of learning process that will be optimal for your child and his peers. The school is the extension of the home, another place where children can learn. So, you have to get your teachers involved in the upbringing of your children.

You want to monitor especially your child's academic performance. The school setup can be a very anxious-filled environment. We have seen how some kids will clam up when they need to speak in front of a class. This can affect very much how they will fare in the different subjects. They may be excellent at the non-verbal parts of the lessons but may do poorly in public speaking. Your goal is not to stop the teachers from doing these activities. There is a good reason why this is done and this will actually benefit your child develop his speaking skills. Coordinate with the teachers so that the process of schooling is not as traumatic.

You also want to watch out for bullying. Socially anxious children are very much prone to bullying because they are different from their peers. Some children will find your child to be eccentric, a cry-baby, a softy, or a mute weakling. Their heightened sensitivity may become the source of laughter of their classmates. Their academic performances may plummet as a result of this bullying. A lot of insecurity and anxiety are developed when the bullying is not addressed. What complicates the problem is that your child will not open up easily to you. They may try to resolve it on their own. You may only know of it when something really bad has happened. It is good that you coordinate with the school when bullying happens. When you feel that your child is being bullied, it is essential that you try to sort out their feelings. They need to feel safe with you to divulge their feelings of hurt and shame. Children need to vent out their repressed feelings or they might implode. The more that you are able to recognize signs of bullying, the earlier you can address the problem.

Chapter 6

Five Phrases to Say to a Socially Anxious Child

—ell—

I truly believe in the power of words. We can say so many things that will affect people intensely. You can use words to hurt other people and to cause a lot of misunderstanding. When you gossip or slander somebody, your words are already hurting other people. But words can also uplift others. When you compliment them for the good things they do or you extend your concern to others, you are sharing a lot of positivity in the world. You can also use words to heal and nurture. In the case of your children, you have to be very careful with your choice of words. When dealing with socially anxious children, you have to remember that you are coming from an area of insecurity. The anxiety and fear are but a mask for the inadequacy they feel inside. As parents, your task is really to get them out of that area of insecurity to an area of confidence, from a position of weakness to a position of strength. If you want to support and change your child, then here are some key phrases you need to say repeatedly to them. The more that they hear these, the more they will be encouraged to be resilient in spite of their anxiety.

"It's ok"

When your child is experiencing a panic attack, you have to tell them "It's ok." These two words can easily calm your child down. Your words actually become a safe zone for them. When you say that "it's ok," you are taking the stress away from them and making the environment safe for them. Your words cushion the impact of stress on your child and he will calm down more easily. When you say these words, you should also be sure that the situation is indeed safe for them. They can relax their defenses and think more rationally when they feel that you are making the environment safe for them.

When you say, "it's ok", you are also acknowledging their feelings. They will feel that their anxiety and fear are not something they imagined but can be conquered. You are validating what they are feeling as true, but also these feelings are also manageable. This is important because there are words and actions that mean to disregard the feelings of your child. When you say to them, "Don't feel anxious, there is nothing to be afraid of," you are saying that what they are feeling is not true. But it is true for them. Recognize the fear and anxiety because that is what they are really feeling. But when you say "It's ok" you are also saying that that anxiety will also pass. Yes, it is there, but they can overcome it.

"You can do it"

You should be the number one cheerleader of your children. It is one thing to think that you are supporting your children, and another to actually say it and show it expressively. Children need to know that their parents approve of them. It might be tiresome for you, but children are in constant need of validation. They want to know if what they are doing is right and pleasing for you. Hence, do not be too stringent in making them feel appreciated. Because of their fear and anxiety, they may feel depressed and disheartened. Words like "You can do it" will uplift their spirits and enable them to keep on trying.

When you say that "You can do it", you are also affirming their giftedness. Because of a lot of bullying, they will be very insecure about their talents and skills. They feel so threatened by other people and by strange environments that they cannot see just how gifted they are. Their anxiety prevents them from expressing their talents. They may actually have good ideas, but because they are afraid to speak in public, they are seen as having weak minds. When you say, "You can do it," you are affirming their gifts and prodding them to share it with others. Instead of focusing on the things that they cannot do, try highlighting all the other things they do well. If they can draw beautifully, affirm that. When they are able to design complicated Lego buildings, celebrate that. When they are able to be confident in one thing, they will be able to be secure in other things. From one place of stability, they can move on to other aspects. They will need just one person who will believe in their giftedness.

"Try again"

When children fail to meet expectations, they are going to feel very down. They will try to please you and meet the goals that you want for them. But sometimes, their fears and anxieties get the best of them. Socially anxious children in particular brood over failure for a long time. They may feel that they are inadequate when they don't meet expectations. Their particular needs supersede their attempts at overcoming their social anxiety. Yes, they want to go to school. Yes, they want to meet new friends. Yes, they want to be able to play with other children and go to places on their own. But somehow, their social awkwardness prevents them from being as sociable as other people. They will try and fail. One time, a second time, a third time, they can be very prone to failure and rejection.

It is during these times that they would need your reassuring support and words. When you tell them "Try again", you are encouraging them to keep on trying. This builds up resilience in children when they know they can start anew each time they fall. More than the number of times that they fall, count the number of times they are willing to try again. It is ok to make mistakes. But it is essential that they try again and again until they succeed. With these words, you are setting the stage for them to become more confident in handling rejection and failure. When they don't meet expectations, it is not the end of the world. There is always a tomorrow where they can continually try. And the more that they try, the more that they will master and conquer their fears. Without these words, they will simply clam up and remain in the house, clinging on to you. But when you prod them to discover the world, they will slowly appreciate the value of trying again.

"I am here"

When you say, "I am here", you are reassuring your child that you are not separating from them and are just within striking distance. This is important when the child is trying to explore new territories. They have to have that assurance of the safe zone, the presence of their attachment figures. This is connected to modeling, wherein you have to be physically present when you enact certain changes in their routine. When you are there, your child will feel comfortable trying a different way of doing things, go a little further from the house, meet new people, and speak to strangers. Even just your physical presence already calms them. You want to tell "I am here" more frequently to them as a sort of mantra they can use even when you are not around. They have to inculcate in their minds that whatever they do, their parents will always be for them.

But you also have to mean this before you say it. You cannot assure them "I am here" when you are always busy doing something else. Of course, you have a life of your own and will need to do many other things aside from raising children. You still need to take care of your business and your work, relate with your colleagues and bosses. You have your own friends to catch up with. You and your husband should always have some time together. And of course, you will need to reserve time for yourself. This is all understandable. But make sure that you reassure your child with your presence in the moments they need you. It may not be always as you have a lot of other aspects to attend to. But in their growing years, try to be there for their milestones. Be there on their first day of school. Be there when they are celebrating school events. Be there when they need someone to talk to. Even if you are busy, spend time with your kids. Only then would "I am here" mean anything to them.

"Be yourself"

Finally, assure your children always that they are wonderful just as they are. Sure, they may be annoying at times. Sure, they may be whiny or prone to tantrums. But at the end of the day, they are still your children. They are beautiful because they come from someone as beautiful as you. It is just that these kids who are extremely shy or have social anxiety have to put up with a lot of fears and insecurity. They are afraid to show their talents and abilities to others. Their shyness prevents them from sharing their wonderful personality with others.

Be sensitive to this. Let your children feel that they can be themselves, whether in your presence or in others. Teach them to stand up to bullying. They may not need to be confrontational, but they have to stand their ground against bullies. You will be able to help them socialize better when you constantly assure them that they are likable just as they are. When you say, "Be yourself," you are celebrating both their giftedness and limitations. You are telling them that they are talented and beautiful just as they are. You are also affirming that they are still in the process of overcoming their shyness and social awkwardness. You are affirming that they are lovable just as they are. And that will go a long way. When children feel they are loved, the anxiety and the fear are kept at bay.

Conclusion

Having children is a blessing. Whoever they may be, whatever qualities they may possess, never forget that children are blessings. They are a fruit of love and you must shower them with love. They in turn will endow you with more love. There may be times that they are difficult to manage, especially when they throw tantrums and become inconsolable. There will be times when you are not at your best, when you feel tired and overworked. During these lows, try to remind yourself that these children are very precious. All of our work is dedicated really to making sure that these children are loved and will have the best chances at a good life.

And being blessings, each child will be different. They have their own temperaments and quirks. They have their own habits and tricks. Some of them will be extremely shy and worry a lot. Some of them may be afraid to speak in public. Some of your children may be afraid to be around strangers. They may have the best ideas, the most imaginative stories, the most precise scientific knowledge contained inside of them.

But because of their social awkwardness, that earth-shaking potential is locked in. The idea of performance or of social interaction dilutes or even completely obliterates that wonderful potential.

And to all these, be patient. Be patient with them until they are able to learn from their mistakes. Be patient as they try out different things at their own pace, however slow it may be. Be patient when they cannot overcome their fears instantly. And most of all, be patient with yourself. Of course, nobody expects you to be the perfect parent. You will have your own mistakes. You will snap sometimes out of frustration. You may lose your cool and insist on your own ways. Be patient with yourself and try again and again to be sensitive parents to your sensitive children. We all need a lot of patience to help us all grow together.

Leaving a Review

As an independent author with limited marketing resources, reviews for my books are essential in order to survive as an indie writer. New works of literature get published daily, so there's no guarantee that any given work will be successful.

Your review can help authors like me grow and share their knowledge with more people. If you enjoyed this book, I would really appreciate your honest feedback. You can leave a review by going to this book's page on Amazon, and clicking "Write A Review."

Leaving an honest review can also help other people find this book easily on Amazon and benefit from it as well. Your feedback is important to me so I can find out what you like and don't, which in turn helps me make better decisions about my writing style.

Thank you,

Freeda

More Books to Consider

Also available in Audiobook format

My good friend, Grace, wrote these books. Please check them out too.

About Author

Freeda is a bestselling author who has written multiple books on parenting and family life. She knows that raising children can be tough, but it's also one of the most rewarding experiences any parent can ever have. She has devoted her life to understanding the psychology behind good parenting and shares what she's learned with others through her books, blogs, and newsletters.

She is also a mother of a highly sensitive child. Freeda shares her story not just to help other parents learn how to raise a highly sensitive child but also to impart lessons on what helped her get through the challenges and live a happy life for both herself and her daughter.

After years of navigating the parenting journey herself, Freeda knows that sharing her life experiences with others could help them on their own parenting journeys. She has helped countless mothers, fathers, grandparents, babysitters, and teachers in making their lives easier by providing sound advice from her extensive experience with children's behavior patterns over the years.

In her free time, she goes to her Yoga and Pilates classes. She also loves baking, especially when requested by her children. Their favorite is her bunch of chewy white chocolate macadamia cookies.

Check out Freeda's profile on Amazon: https://www.amazon.com/author/freedameighan

References

Bianca Acevedo, Elaine Aron, Sarah Pospos and Dana Jessen, The functional highly sensitive brain: a review of the brain circuits underlying sensory processing sensitivity and seemingly related disorders, Philosophical Transactions of the Royal Society B: Biological Sciences, 10.1098/rstb.2017.0161, 373, 1744, (20170161), (2018).

American Psychiatric Association. (2013). Diagnostic and statistical manual of mental disorders (DSM-5®). American Psychiatric Pub.

Made in the USA
Monee, IL
01 December 2021